CHRIS SINGLETON
AND
DEAN BURRELL

# BASEBALL

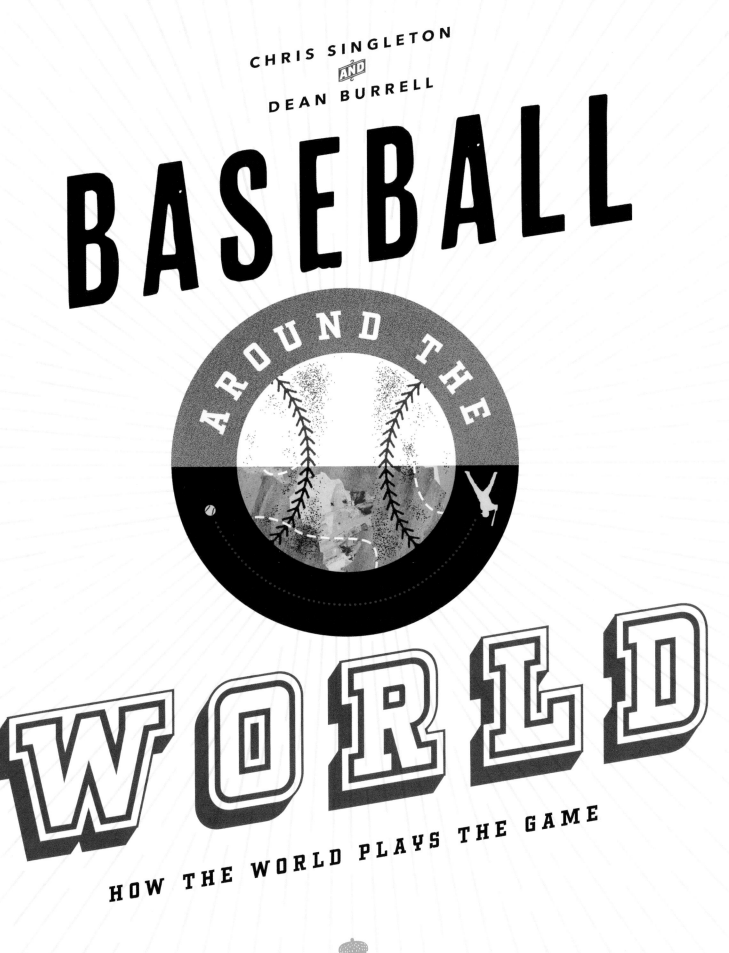

AROUND THE

# WORLD

HOW THE WORLD PLAYS THE GAME

BUSHEL & PECK BOOKS

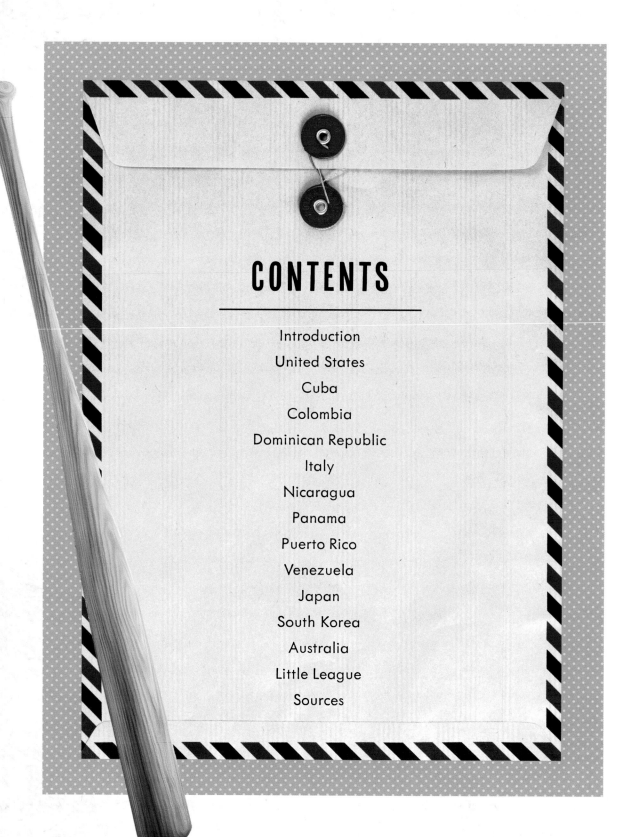

# CONTENTS

**BUSHEL & PECK BOOKS**

Text copyright © 2022 by Chris Singleton and Dean Burrell

Published by Bushel & Peck Books, www.bushelandpeckbooks.com.

All rights reserved. No part of this publication may be reproduced without written permission from the publisher.

Bushel & Peck Books is dedicated to fighting illiteracy all over the world. For every book we sell, we donate one to a child in need—book for book. To nominate a school or organization to receive free books, please visit www.bushelandpeckbooks.com.

Type set in Metallophile Sp8, Cheap Pine, Avenir Next, and Abril Display.

LCCN: 2022933618

ISBN: 9781638190912

First Edition

Printed in Canada

10 9 8 7 6 5 4 3 2 1

# INTRODUCTION

> *"Get out the rye bread and mustard, grandma, 'cause it's grand salami time!"*
>
> **—DAVE NIEHAUS, LONGTIME SEATTLE MARINERS ANNOUNCER**

People often think of baseball as an American sport. Terms such as "America's pastime" and the "boys of summer" bring up images of warm summer nights in small towns. Yes, the game we think of—that we know and love—is rooted in the sandlots and Little League fields across the U.S. But baseball is so much bigger. In many ways, baseball really is a world sport.

Many baseball stars we're familiar with come from foreign countries, hoping to play alongside their American counterparts. At the beginning of the 2021 season, 256 Major League players were foreign-born. These players represented twenty different countries. They also accounted for an impressive 28 percent of the players who took to the fields on Opening Day. As these players improved their skills back home, they often rose to become national heroes. For instance, before he achieved fame in the U.S., Ichiro Suzuki already had a successful career in Japan. When he left to join the Seattle Mariners, the fans back home didn't see it as a loss. Instead, their pride grew even bigger. Ichiro showed the world how great Japanese baseball was. This national pride exists everywhere, and players hope to one day represent their home country on the world stage. Indeed, in 2006 the World Baseball Classic was formed to celebrate how far the game had traveled around the globe.

One of the great things about the game is that it shows people how we are all equal. Baseball is shared all over. Here in the U.S., for instance, you can travel to just about any city and see someone wearing a Boston Red Sox cap. Or mention the Chicago Cubs, and someone nearby will surely sigh, "Maybe next year." And when you travel outside the country, you'll see the New York Yankees logo pretty much everywhere you go. It's one of the most recognized logos around the world. Even though you may not speak Spanish or Japanese or Italian, that cap with the logo means you have something in common with the locals.

After losing my mom back in 2015, my mission became one of unity and of celebrating our differences. Over time, I realized how important it is to remind people that, at the end of the day, we are a lot more alike than we are different. And baseball, my first love, proves this perfectly. As you read this book and learn about baseball around the world, you'll see just how much the game unifies us. Regardless of our differences, our love for the game of baseball is all the same!

—Chris Singleton

## HOW BASEBALL ARRIVED

The game of baseball dates back to the English colonists coming to America. In the mid-1700s, several games developed in England that involved a batter hitting a ball and then running around bases. The colonists brought these games with them. In the mid-1800s, as the games continued to change, a sport developed in New York City that became the game we think of today. Baseball was still an amateur sport back then, meaning that players weren't getting paid to play. That all changed in 1869, when the Cincinnati Red Stockings began charging admission for fans to watch the games and the players were paid salaries.

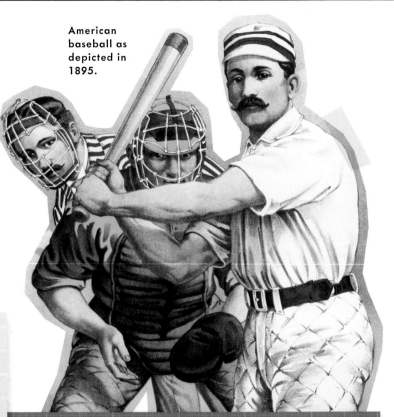

American baseball as depicted in 1895.

## THE COLOR BARRIER

*Before Jackie Robinson (pictured left) broke the MLB color barrier or Larry Doby became the first Black player in the American League, many players in the Negro Leagues spent playing time in Cuba, Mexico, Puerto Rico, and other Latin American countries. Some played winter ball in the off-season in order to keep in shape. Others were attracted by the higher salaries. But beyond the playing time and the money, the reason the players often left the U.S. was lack of inclusion. In Latin America, the Black players did not have to face racism or segregation. After they played side by side with the white and Hispanic players, they could all go to dinner together and stay in the same hotels.*

## WHAT IT'S LIKE TODAY

Professional baseball has been around for 150 years. From the beginning, Major League Baseball (MLB) has looked for ways to expand its reach, both at home and, later, abroad. Today, MLB has people working in Asia, Europe, and Latin America. Their job is to help people of all ages enjoy the sport. In addition, individual MLB teams have permanent training camps outside the U.S. Indeed, all thirty teams have training facilities in the Dominican Republic.

In Major League clubhouses, it's also common for the coaches to speak Spanish. Since nearly one third of players come from Latin America, every MLB team has a Spanish-speaking coach. As Chicago White Sox manager Tony LaRussa puts it, "If you seriously aspire to be a manager . . . you must practice Spanish." Even when the Hispanic players are fluent in English, speaking Spanish with them is a great advantage. It lets them know that they and their heritage are respected.

Left: Fenway Park, home of the Boston Red Sox since 1912, is the nation's oldest stadium.

A BRIEF | 1786: Earliest known mention of baseball. / 1800s: Teams begin to form. | 1901: American League is formed.
1857: National Association of Base Ball Players becomes first major league. | 1903: First World Series is played.

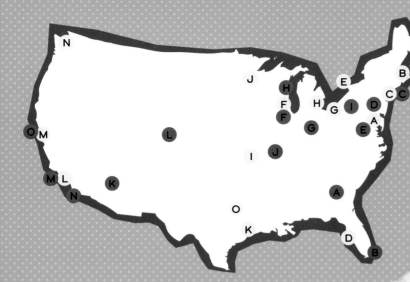

## AMERICAN LEAGUE

| | |
|---|---|
| A | Baltimore Orioles |
| B | Boston Red Sox |
| C | New York Yankees |
| D | Tampa Bay Rays |
| E | Toronto Blue Jays |
| F | Chicago White Sox |
| G | Cleveland Guardians |
| H | Detroit Tigers |
| I | Kansas City Royals |
| J | Minnesota Twins |
| K | Houston Astros |
| L | Los Angeles Angels |
| M | Oakland Athletics |
| N | Seattle Mariners |
| O | Texas Rangers |

## NATIONAL LEAGUE

| | |
|---|---|
| A | Atlanta Braves |
| B | Miami Marlins |
| C | New York Mets |
| D | Philadelphia Phillies |
| E | Washington Nationals |
| F | Chicago Cubs |
| G | Cincinnati Reds |
| H | Milwaukee Brewers |
| I | Pittsburgh Pirates |
| J | St. Louis Cardinals |
| K | Arizona Diamondbacks |
| L | Colorado Rockies |
| M | Los Angeles Dodgers |
| N | San Diego Padres |
| O | San Francisco Giants |

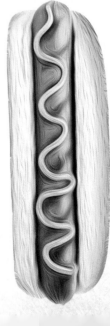

Right: Babe Ruth, still one of America's most famous players of all time.

# GIVING BACK

Baseball is a game of teamwork and community. The players on the field never forget where they come from. Albert Pujols's foundation works to improve the quality of life for the people of the Dominican Republic, where Albert grew up. From players who open youth baseball camps (Cal Ripken Jr.) to those who give generously to disaster relief (Ichiro Suzuki), the list of players who give back is a long one.

**Albert Pujols**          **Cal Ripken Jr.**

# WOMEN IN BASEBALL

*Since its earliest days as an amateur sport, baseball has mostly been reserved for men. Indeed, as late as the 1970s, people believed that the game was too rough for women. That thinking is changing. Starting in 2022, MLB teams included two dozen women coaches. Elsewhere in the world, 2022 saw the first time a woman took the field in a professional game.*

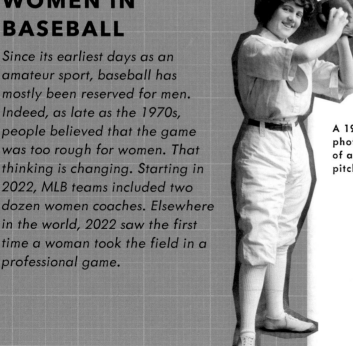

A 1913 photograph of a woman pitcher.

# FESTIVE FOOD

*Pop quiz: When you go to a ball game, what do you look for first? If you said hot dogs and cotton candy, you're not alone. These days, however, fans have a huge number of food options that reflect the many cultures that are found locally as well as on the field. At Oracle Park in San Francisco, for instance, everyone loves the Cha-Cha Bowl at Orlando's Caribbean BBQ (named after Orlando Cepeda, a Giants legend and proud Puerto Rican).*

# CUBA

## HOW BASEBALL ARRIVED

Baseball was introduced to Latin America in the mid-1800s, and the Cuban League was one of the first to form outside the United States. In 1864, after attending college in Alabama, two brothers returned to their Cuban home. Nemesio and Ernesto Guilló brought with them a bat and ball and a love of the game. Within four years, they established the Habana (Havana) Baseball Club. In 1878, another pair of brothers, who had studied in New York City, returned to the island and formed the Almendares Baseball Club. The two clubs became rivals, and a Cuban baseball league was established. Over the next eighty years, baseball thrived on the island.

Cuban baseball cards from 1909.

EMILIO PALOMINO R. F.

P. BEBE

Right: The 1911 Habana team.

1—Gonzalo Sanchez, catcher. 2—Sam Lloyd, short stop. 3—Ricardo Hernandez, outfielder. 4—Preston Hill, outfielder. 5—Grant Johnson, short stop y second base. 6—Luis Padron, right fielder. 7—J. H. Magri-nat, outfielder. 8—Carlos Moran, third base. 9—Camilo Valdes, mascota. JUGADORES DEL "HABANA."

## WHAT IT'S LIKE TODAY

Baseball is more than just a game for Cubans—it's part of their national identity. The game is widespread across the country. The Cuban National League is actually made up of many different leagues. The main competition takes place between the island's provinces and is called the Cuban National Series (Serie Nacional de Béisbol, or SNB). Sixteen teams play more than ninety games each during the season. All of the players are amateurs, and they play for the province where they were born.

The stadium in Camagüey.

## IMPOSSIBLE DECISIONS

Fidel Castro, leader of Cuba from 1959 to 2008.

In 1960, after the Cuban Revolution, President Fidel Castro (shown right) banned all professional sports. He believed that an athlete's success, at any level, should be a benefit to the country and not the individual. This ban meant that athletes could no longer make a living just by playing the games they loved. As a result, many Cuban baseball players were forced to make a hard decision: stay and play at home for little money, or try to defect to a neighboring country, leaving their home and loved ones behind. Many chose to leave, including such MLB stars as brothers Livan and Orlando "El Duque" Hernandez, Aroldis Chapman, Yoenis Cespedes, Yasiel Puig, and Jose Abreu.

A BRIEF TIMELINE OF BASEBALL IN CUBA

1868: Guilló brothers establish the Habana Baseball Club.

1878: Cuban League is founded.

1899: "All Cubans" team becomes first Latin American team to tour U.S.

| 1850 | 1860 | 1870 | 1880 | 1890 | 1900 | 1910 | 1920 | 1930 |

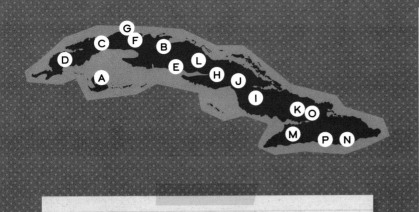

| TEAM | CITY |
|------|------|
| A Isla de la Juventud | Nuevo Gerona |
| B Matanzas | Matanzas |
| C Artemisa | Artemisa |
| D Pinar del Río | Pinar del Río |
| E Cienfuegos | Cienfuegos |
| F Mayabeque | San José de las Lajas |
| G Industriales | Ciudad de La Habana |
| H Sancti Spíritus | Sancti Spíritus |
| I Camagüey | Camagüey |
| J Ciego de Ávila | Ciego de Ávila |
| K Las Tunas | Las Tunas |
| L Villa Clara | Santa Clara |
| M Granma | Bayamo |
| N Guantánamo | Guantánamo |
| O Holguín | Holguín |
| P Santiago de Cuba | Santiago de Cuba |

## THE CUBAN GREATS

It's hard to think of MLB and not include the Cuban greats. Stars such as Luis Tiant (Boston Red Sox) and Tony Perez (Cincinnati Reds) are just a couple who hometown fans will always remember. Today, Cuban players are found throughout MLB. In fact, there are so many stars that you could field a whole lineup with just Cubans. When the Chicago White Sox took the field in 2021, four of their regular starters were from Cuba. White Sox fans are especially proud of Jose Abreu, their first baseman and a team leader. (Jose won the American League MVP Award in 2020.)

## ROOT, ROOT, ROOT FOR THE HOME TEAM

Attending baseball games in Cuba is lots of fun. The fans know a lot about the game and the teams, and they pay close attention the whole time. Food and drinks are scarce, and the seating is often just on benches. But admission is typically free, and the stands are packed with cheering fans. Whenever a run scores, the whole team lines up on the field to slap hands with the runner.

## CUBAN SLUGGER

Did you know? Cuban-born Jose Canseco (above) was the first foreign player to reach the four-hundred-home-runs plateau in the MLB.

After the fifth inning the umpires are treated to ice water or lemonade, brought out to them on a tray.

1961: Fidel Castro replaces professional baseball with amateur leagues.

1999: Baltimore Orioles play the Cuban national team in first MLB-Cuba exhibition game since 1959.

2019: Matthew McLaughlin becomes first American to play for Cuban team in over 60 years.

1940    1950    1960    1970    1980    1990    2000    2010    2020    2030

# COLOMBIA

| QUICK STATS | YEAR STARTED | NUMBER OF TEAMS | PERMANENT STADIUMS |
|---|---|---|---|
| | 1870s | 6 | 12 |

## HOW BASEBALL ARRIVED

Baseball arrived in the South American country of Colombia in the 1870s and quickly took hold. Throughout the 1900s, the game became more and more popular as the players improved their skills. In 1947, the Colombian national team won the Amateur World Series. This international tournament included teams from the Caribbean as well as Central and South America. After this success, the following year the Colombian League was formed. However, it took until the 1990s for the sport to really take off—at last, several Colombian stars joined the MLB.

## BEST IN CLASS

*Did you know? Orlando Cabrera, an infielder for the Montreal Expos (now the Washington Nationals), is considered by some to be the best shortstop the team has ever had.*

## WHAT IT'S LIKE TODAY

Today, the Colombian Professional Baseball League (Liga Colombiana de Béisbol Profesional, or LCBP) is made up of six teams. The teams play during the winter months, from October through December, and each team plays fifty games. At the end of the regular season, the top four teams play a series of playoff games. The top two teams then play in the League Championship, and the champion later takes part in the Caribbean World Series (Serie del Caribe). The Caribbean Series takes place in February and is the top baseball tournament in Latin America.

**A BRIEF TIMELINE OF BASEBALL IN COLOMBIA**

1870s: Baseball is first introduced.

1897: Baseball begins in Cartagena, a future powerhouse city for MLB players.

1850    1860    1870    1880    1890    1900    1910    1920    1930

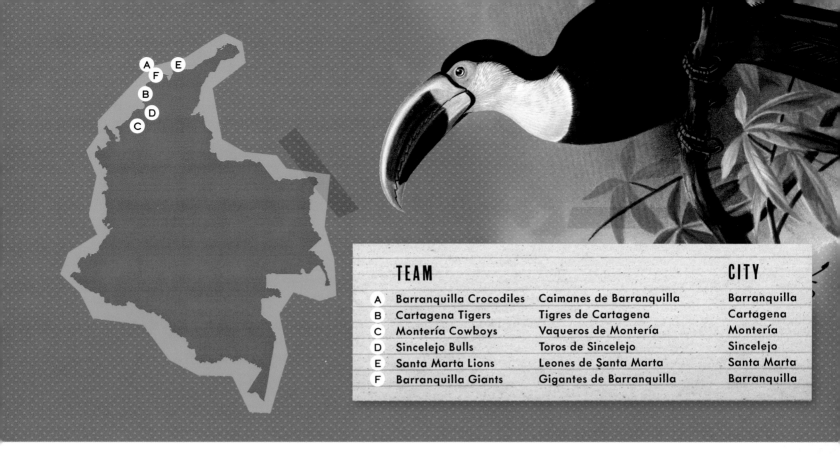

| TEAM | | CITY |
|------|---|------|
| A Barranquilla Crocodiles | Caimanes de Barranquilla | Barranquilla |
| B Cartagena Tigers | Tigres de Cartagena | Cartagena |
| C Montería Cowboys | Vaqueros de Montería | Montería |
| D Sincelejo Bulls | Toros de Sincelejo | Sincelejo |
| E Santa Marta Lions | Leones de Santa Marta | Santa Marta |
| F Barranquilla Giants | Gigantes de Barranquilla | Barranquilla |

## COLOMBIANS IN THE MAJORS

*Starting in the 1990s, Colombian players have really made a name for themselves in the MLB. In 1996, a shortstop named Edgar Renteria took the field for the Florida Marlins. Edgar went on to play in three World Series and was an All-Star five times. Among today's players, MLB has nearly a dozen Colombians taking the field. Look for Donovan Solano (Cincinnati Reds), Nabil Crismatt (San Diego Padres), and Giovanny Urshela (Minnesota Twins).*

Carlos González          Johan Santana

1947: Colombia wins the Amateur World Series.
1948: Colombian League is formed.

2010: Two new teams added to the league.

2019: Two more teams added.

2020: Colombia first appears in the Caribbean Series.

1940   1950   1960   1970   1980   1990   2000   2010   2020   2030

# DOMINICAN REPUBLIC

## HOW BASEBALL ARRIVED

No one is exactly sure how or when baseball arrived in the Dominican Republic. Some say it came with Cuban migrants in the late 1800s. Other people believe it was the American marines, who played the game in their spare time when the U.S. occupied the country in the early 1900s. No matter how it arrived, the locals quickly adopted the game as their own. Professional baseball officially began in 1951.

Did you know? Sammy Sosa was the first foreign-born player to hit five hundred home runs!

## WHAT IT'S LIKE TODAY

For Dominicans, loving baseball means loving their country. And for the youth, baseball is both a dream and a hope for the future—a chance to add their name to the long list of Dominican legends who have played the game. The Dominican Republic Professional Baseball League (Liga de Béisbol Profesional de la República Dominicana, or LIDOM) is made up of six teams. The season runs from October through January, and each team plays fifty games before the playoffs begin. Finally, the top two teams play for the national title, and the winner later competes in the Caribbean World Series.

República Dominicana Correos 6¢
VI JUEGOS DEPORTIVOS NACIONALES SAN PEDRO DE MACORIS-83

## CARIBBEAN WORLD SERIES

The Caribbean World Series (Serie del Caribe) is the highest tournament of professional baseball in Latin America. Currently, six countries send their best teams— their league champions—to compete. The participating countries include Colombia, Dominican Republic, Mexico, Panama, Puerto Rico, and Venezuela. (Cuba was a past participant but dropped out in 2019.) The series is played in February, after the various league champions are determined. Its location rotates each year among the countries.

---

**A BRIEF TIMELINE OF BASEBALL IN THE DOMINICAN REPUBLIC**

1870s: Cuban migrants introduce baseball.

1890: First two clubs (Ozama and Nuevo) are formed.

1907: Licey club is added.

| 1850 | 1860 | 1870 | 1880 | 1890 | 1900 | 1910 | 1920 | 1930 |

| TEAM | CITY |
|------|------|
| (A) Águilas Cibaeñas | Santiago |
| (B) Estrellas Orientales | San Pedro de Macorís |
| (C) Gigantes del Cibao | San Francisco de Macorís |
| (D) Leones del Escogido | Santo Domingo |
| (E) Tigres del Licey | Santo Domingo |
| (F) Toros del Este | La Romana |

## MLB-BOUND

*The Dominican Republic sends more players to the MLB than any other country. Since the mid-1950s, more than 700 Dominicans have played in the majors! Such greats as Sammy Sosa, Pedro Martinez, David Ortiz, and Albert Pujols are now household names. Among the nearly 100 Dominicans starting today, look for Fernando Tatís Jr. (San Diego Padres) and Starling Marte (New York Mets).*

Young fans of the game at practice.

1937: Stars from U.S. Negro leagues visit.

1948: National team wins gold in Baseball World Cup.
1951: Dominican League (today's modern league) is formed.

2013: National team wins World Baseball Classic undefeated.

1940   1950   1960   1970   1980   1990   2000   2010   2020   2030

# ITALY

## HOW BASEBALL ARRIVED

In 1919, a young Italian named Max Otto brought his love of the game home after living in America. In the 1920s, Max helped to form two teams—mostly made up of university students—and interest began to grow as the teams faced each other. The sport really took off in the 1940s, however, during and after World War II. When American soldiers were sent to Italy, U.S. President Franklin Roosevelt saw to it that their supplies included bats and balls. As the troops marched across the countryside, the locals learned how great America's pastime was. Immediately after the war, Max Otto founded Italy's first baseball league in Milan.

The U.S. Navy and Army play an exhibition game in Italy in 1918.

## WHAT IT'S LIKE TODAY

Both baseball and softball are very popular in Italy, and the two are governed by the Italian Baseball Softball Federation (Federazione Italiana Baseball Softball, or FIBS). The league has thirty-two teams that are divided into eight groups. The team with the best record from each group advances into the playoffs. The two best teams finally compete in the Italian Baseball Series, and the champion earns a prize called the scudetto. The full season runs April through August.

*Scudetto* in Italian means "championship badge" or, literally, "little shield." Every sport in Italy awards its champion the scudetto. Each team that wins its championship proudly wears the scudetto on their jerseys or uniforms.

## THE CITY OF BASEBALL

Baseball stadiums in Italy vary greatly. Most stands hold about 2,000 to 3,000 fans, but some can be tiny (just 200 seats). Nettuno, a city on the coast about forty-three miles from Rome, is called "the city of baseball." This is where baseball in Italy landed, literally. (During World War II, American troops landed on the nearby beaches.) The stadium here is by far the biggest, with seating for 8,000.

Italy's largest baseball stadium is located in Nettuno, the "city of baseball."

A BRIEF TIMELINE OF BASEBALL

**1889:** Spalding World Tour exposes Italy to baseball.

**1919:** Max Otto establishes baseball.

| TEAM | | CITY |
|---|---|---|
| A | UnipolSai Fortitudo | Bologna |
| B | Collecchio Baseball | Collecchio |
| C | Macerata Angels | Macerata |
| D | Parma Clima | Parma |
| E | Godo Baseball | Russi |
| F | San Marino Baseball | San Marino |

## THE BEST IN EUROPE

*Italy is at the top of the list of best baseball leagues in Europe (it shares this achievement with the Netherlands). Its national baseball team has been crowned the European champion ten times. Even with this success, only about a half dozen players from Italy have made it to the MLB. But that's not to say that Italians in America have had no impact. Joe DiMaggio, for instance, is considered to be one of the best to ever play the game. While the folks in Europe celebrate the achievements of the countless Italian Americans playing the game today, the players in the U.S. are openly proud of their heritage.*

Joe DiMaggio, one of the greatest players in baseball history, was born in California to Sicilian Italian immigrants.

## SNACK BREAK

*Food concessions vary in Italy. Depending on the stadium, fans can probably find peanuts and popcorn. Even so, Italian baseball fans are more likely to order espresso drinks and panini sandwiches. No matter. The one treat that everyone enjoys? GELATO!*

# NICARAGUA

## HOW BASEBALL ARRIVED

Everywhere you go in Nicaragua, you'll find people playing baseball. The game was introduced in the 1880s by an American businessman named Albert Addlesberg. At the time, much of the Caribbean was influenced by the British (who had colonies there). With the British came another game using bats and balls: cricket. Addlesberg was such a baseball fan that he convinced two of the cricket clubs to switch sports. Later, when the United States took control of the country, the American troops built ball fields and taught people how to play. When Addlesberg shipped in equipment from the United States, baseball arrived; when the U.S. forces came, the game quickly spread. But the country was politically troubled. In 1967, professional baseball came to a halt when the dictator pulled its funding. Still, baseball remained popular. The Nicaraguans loved it.

Top: A baseball team from the U.S. Marine Corp plays in Managua, Nicaragua, in 1915.

*"Many [Latinos] come from a different country, a poor Third World country, where there's a lot of need. There are a lot of people that live in poverty that just need to have an opportunity, the chance. And where better than [the United States]? And for that we are grateful to this country, for allowing us to come here and do what we love to do, which is play baseball."*

**—DENNIS MARTINEZ, NICARAGUAN PITCHING GREAT**

## WHAT IT'S LIKE TODAY

In 2004, baseball returned to Nicaragua. Today, the Nicaraguan Professional Baseball League (La Liga de Beisbol Profesional Nacional, or LBPN) has five teams. Each team plays thirty games over a season that takes place in November. The top four teams advance to the playoffs, and the top two go to the championship.

Young fans attend an LBPN game.

**A BRIEF TIMELINE OF BASEBALL IN NICARAGUA**

1880s: Businessman Albert Addlesberg introduces baseball.

1887: First two teams are formed.

1904: First continuous team is formed.

1850   1860   1870   1880   1890   1900   1910   1920   1930

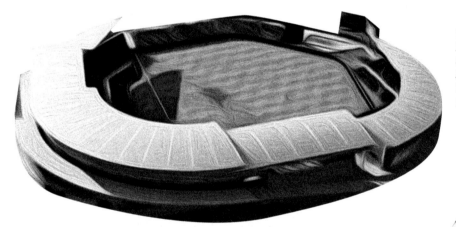

## TOP PLAYERS

*The most famous player is surely Dennis Martinez. He was the first Nicaraguan to play in the MLB. Martinez made his debut in 1976 as a pitcher for the Baltimore Orioles. Among today's top players, look for Jonathan Loáisiga (New York Yankees). Jonathan began his pitching career in 2018 and quickly became one of the hardest-throwing in the game. His pitches average ninety-eight miles per hour!*

**Jonathan Loáisiga**

| | TEAM | CITY |
|---|---|---|
| A | Indios del Bóer | Managua |
| B | Tigres del Chinandega | Chinandega |
| C | Gigantes de Rivas | Rivas |
| D | Leones de León | León |
| E | Tren del Norte | Esteli |

The Dennis Martinez Stadium in Managua can hold 30,000 people!

## THE CROWD GOES WILD!

*Nicaraguans are baseball-crazy. Go to a stadium today, and you'll see cheerleaders, mascots, and even marching bands that play throughout the game. Fans don't come to sit and watch quietly. They love their favorite teams, and they show it with loud enthusiasm.*

For twenty-two years, Dennis Martinez was a league-leading pitcher.

Did you know? In the 1996 Summer Olympics in Atlanta, the Nicaraguan team made it into the semifinals. They narrowly lost the bronze medal to Japan.

1956: LBPN league is formed.

1967: League is closed.

1996: Presidential candidates promise funding for a national team.

2004: LBPN is reestablished and professional baseball resumes.

1940   1950   1960   1970   1980   1990   2000   2010   2020   2030

# PANAMA

## HOW BASEBALL ARRIVED

**M**any believe that baseball came to Panama in the early 1900s, when the United States crafted a treaty with Panama to finish building the Panama Canal. (The waterway would connect the Atlantic and Pacific oceans.) But before the U.S. arrived, Panama was ruled by Colombia. It was the Colombians, in fact, who introduced the game to the country as early as 1883. Still, when thousands of American workers came later, the sport quickly grew. The locals had a passion for the game, and in the 1940s they formed their first professional league.

Above: A baseball game underway in Panama in 1913.
Below: Construction on the Panama Canal in 1913.

## WHAT IT'S LIKE TODAY

The Panama Professional League (Liga Profesional de Béisbol de Panamá, or Probeis) is made up of four teams. The teams play a short season over the winter, and the champion goes on to play in the Caribbean Series.

Kids practice baseball in a small town in Panama.

**A BRIEF TIMELINE OF**

1883: Colombians introduce baseball to Panama.

1900s: American canal workers popularize the game.

1916: MLB considers Panama as a possible winter training site.

## HALL-OF-FAME PITCHER

*At the top of the list of national baseball heroes is Mariano Rivera (below). Raised in a small village, Mariano (or Mo, for short) worked on his father's fishing boat and played baseball in his spare time. His baseball gloves were often made out of cardboard. A scout for the New York Yankees recognized Mo's pitching talent and signed him up quickly. His first contract was for $2,000. The Yankees gave him a new pair of shoes and a real glove. Mariano tells about how he cried at night because he couldn't speak English to talk with his teammates. But he didn't give up. For the next nineteen seasons, Mariano dominated as a relief pitcher. When he was voted into the Baseball Hall of Fame in 2019, he received votes from every ballot—he became the first player ever to be selected unanimously.*

|   | TEAM | CITY |
|---|------|------|
| A | Astronautas de Chiriquí | Los Santos |
| B | Toros de Herrera | Chitré |
| C | Aguilas Metropolitanas | Panamá |
| D | Federales de Chiriquí | Chiriquí |

Rod grew up hitting bottle caps with broomsticks.

## HEAVY HITTER

*The ballparks in Panama are all pretty small. They hold between 2,000 and 5,000 fans. The biggest stadium, however, seats 25,000. Rod Carew National Stadium (Estadio Nacional de Panama) is named after one of the best Major League hitters of all time. Rod Carew (shown right) sealed Panama's place in MLB history and became the all-time batting leader for the Minnesota Twins.*

# PUERTO RICO

 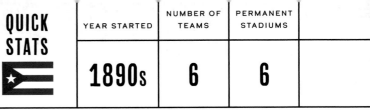
## HOW BASEBALL ARRIVED

**W**hen baseball was introduced to Puerto Rico, at the very end of the 19th century, the locals were unimpressed. A group of Puerto Ricans and Cubans who had learned to play in the United States formed the first two teams and began playing games together. Years later, American troops stationed on the island organized games against locals to fill their spare time. When the Puerto Rican teams beat the Americans, the newspapers happily reported the results. Baseball became popular. The game was taught in schools, and every town had a team that played on Sundays and holidays. In 1938, the first baseball league was formed.

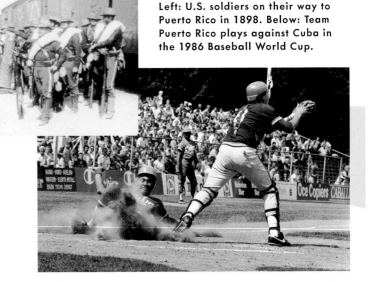

Left: U.S. soldiers on their way to Puerto Rico in 1898. Below: Team Puerto Rico plays against Cuba in the 1986 Baseball World Cup.

## WHAT IT'S LIKE TODAY

In 2012, the league chose to honor Puerto Rican baseball legend Roberto Clemente. The league's official name was changed to Liga de Béisbol Profesional Roberto Clemente (LBPRC). But people just call it the Puerto Rican Winter League. Every year, from November through January, baseball heats up on the island. In addition to the local players, many MLB players come down from the U.S. to keep in shape in their off-season.

The league is made up of five teams, and each team plays a thirty-game season. Playoffs take place starting in January, leading up to the league championship. The season's champion later competes in the Caribbean World Series (Serie del Caribe).

Orlando Cepeda

Roberto Alomar

*"For me, I'm very happy to represent Puerto Rico and to do a good job for my country. It's always very nice when you represent where you're from."*

**—IVAN RODRIGUEZ, HALL OF FAME CATCHER**

Some consider Ivan Rodriguez to be the best MLB catcher in all of baseball.

**A BRIEF TIMELINE OF BASEBALL IN PUERTO RICO**

1890s: A group of Puerto Ricans and Cubans introduce baseball.
1897: First two teams are formed.

1898: Puerto Rico becomes a territory of the U.S., and American soldiers organize a baseball club.

| 1850 | 1860 | 1870 | 1880 | 1890 | 1900 | 1910 | 1920 | 1930 |

# ISLAND SUPERSTARS

Since the 1940s, more than 200 Puerto Ricans have played in the MLB. Among the many greats on the field today, you'll find Javier Baez (Detroit Tigers), Francisco Lindor (New York Mets), Jose Berrios (Toronto Blue Jays), and Yadier Molina (St. Louis Cardinals). Speaking of Yadier, he's the youngest of three Molina brothers who have played catcher at the professional level. All three have earned World Series rings—two apiece, to be exact.

Over the years, four Puerto Ricans have been selected for the baseball Hall of Fame— Roberto Clemente, Orlando Cepeda, Roberto Alomar, and Ivan Rodriguez. In his induction ceremony speech, Ivan spoke of his national pride, as well as the importance of following your dreams:

"Don't let anyone say your dreams cannot be accomplished. Tell them about a short kid who would hang from a rope for hours, dangling there, trying to stretch himself and hoping to become as tall as the other boys. . . . That was me . . . and obviously, it didn't work. But I did get a cool nickname out of it: Pudge."

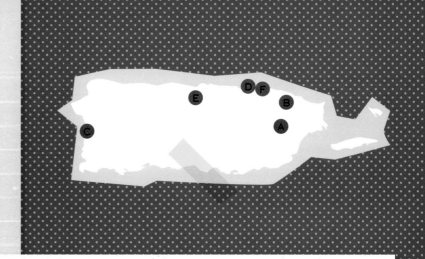

| | TEAM | | CITY |
|---|---|---|---|
| A | Caguas Creoles | Criollos de Caguas | Caguas |
| B | Carolina Giants | Gigantes de Carolina | Carolina |
| C | Mayagüez Indians | Indios de Mayagüez | Mayagüez |
| D | Santurce Crabbers | Cangrejeros de Santurce | San Juan |
| E | Manatí Athenians | Atenienses de Manatí | Manatí |
| F | RA12 | RA12 | San Juan |

## REMEMBERING ROBERTO CLEMENTE

The Roberto Clemente Award is given each year to the MLB player who shows extraordinary character and community involvement. Clemente (left) died tragically in a plane crash on New Year's Eve while delivering aid to earthquake victims in Nicaragua.

A postage stamp from Nicaragua honoring Clemente.

"[Roberto Clemente] was an icon for the Spanish-speaking players because what he showed was humanity. Not just because he was a baseball player, but because he was a family man, and he was able to leave his family behind just to help a different country."

—DENNIS MARTINEZ, NICARAGUAN PITCHING GREAT

1938: First league is founded.

1951: National team wins World Cup.

1971: Roberto Clemente becomes first Puerto Rican included in Baseball Hall of Fame.

2001: MLB opening day game is held in San Juan, Puerto Rico.

1940    1950    1960    1970    1980    1990    2000    2010    2020    2030

# VENEZUELA

## HOW BASEBALL ARRIVED

Baseball in Venezuela owes its rise in importance to both Cuba and the United States. In the late 1800s, a Cuban cigar factory opened in the country. The Cuban employees played ball games in their spare time and began to teach the locals. A couple decades later, American oil workers arrived in the country. (Venezuela is one of the world's largest oil producers.) As more and more oil workers came, interest in baseball spread quickly among the locals.

In 1941, the Venezuela national team beat Cuba in the Amateur World Series. This victory was a huge achievement, as it showed how skilled the Venezuelans were. The players became national heroes overnight—they were known as Los Héroes del '41 (The Heroes of '41)—and baseball fever exploded. The Venezuelan Professional Baseball League (Liga Venezolana de Béisbol Profesional, or LVPB) was formed in 1945.

Top: An early Venezuelan team from Caracas. Right: Players practice in 1895.

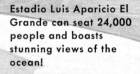

Estadio Luis Aparicio El Grande can seat 24,000 people and boasts stunning views of the ocean!

## WHAT IT'S LIKE TODAY

The Venezuelan league is considered a winter league. Its season runs from mid-October through December. Eight teams play sixty-three games each during the regular season, and the top five teams enter the playoffs. The top teams then play a round-robin series of games to determine the top two, who will play for the championship at the end of January. The champion later competes in the Caribbean World Series (Serie del Caribe).

| TEAM | | CITY |
|---|---|---|
| A | Anzoátegui Caribbeans | Puerto la Cruz |
| B | Aragua Tigers | Maracay |
| C | Caracas Lions | Caracas |
| D | La Guaira Sharks | Caracas |
| E | Lara Cardinals | Barquisimeto |
| F | Magallanes Navigators | Valencia |
| G | Margarita Braves | Margarita |
| H | Zulia Eagles | Maracaibo |

Miguel Cabrera was signed at just age sixteen!

Carlos González

Johan Santana

# BASEBALL POWERHOUSE

Of the Latin American countries, Venezuela sends the second-highest number of players to the MLB. (The Dominican Republic sends the most.) In 2021 alone, sixty-four players were on the Opening Day rosters. Famous players such as Félix Hernández (fans called him "King Felix"), Carlos González ("CarGo"), and Johan Santana put up league-leading stats year after year. Today, fans get to be amazed by such stars as Salvador Pérez (Kansas City Royals) and Miguel Cabrera (Detroit Tigers), among many others.

A favorite Venezuelan snack is arepa, a sandwich made from two cornmeal patties and a delicious filling.

## HALL OF FAMER

Luis Aparicio became the first Venezuelan professional baseball player inducted into the National Baseball Hall of Fame. Baseball legend Ted Williams called Aparicio the best shortstop he had ever seen.

## TURN UP THE NOISE!

Venezuelan fans are obsessed with baseball. Most fans wear team jerseys to the ballpark, and many wear their hats and team T-shirts even not on game days. The ball games are loud, with a party atmosphere. One fan described that the crowd moves in unison as the people dance to the music playing over the speakers. Fans openly show their delight when their team is playing—smiling and clapping—and some even weep when their team is losing.

# JAPAN

## HOW BASEBALL ARRIVED

A 1934 poster promoting Babe Ruth's tour in Japan.

Around 1872, an English teacher in Japan saw that his students needed more exercise. The American teacher, Horace Wilson, also had a great love for baseball. So, he taught the students how to play. But the students struggled to understand the rules. Several years later, a Japanese railway engineer named Hiraoka Hiroshi returned to the country after studying in the U.S. He, too, brought back a love of the game. He also brought some official rulebooks. Hiroshi helped to translate the finer points of the sport. Because of his efforts, baseball in Japan quickly took hold.

In 1934, a team of American all stars, including Babe Ruth, traveled across the ocean. The games played against the local teams were hugely popular. The Japanese were so impressed by the skills of the American players that they soon formed the Japanese Professional Baseball League. The first team was the Yomiuri Giants. By 1950, the league had grown so big that it needed to split into two. It also renamed itself the Nippon Professional Baseball League (NPB).

An early Japanese baseball card, called *menko*, from around 1948.

## WHAT IT'S LIKE TODAY

The NPB today has twelve teams. The league is divided into two divisions—Pacific and Central. Each team plays 144 games over a season, followed by playoffs that lead to the championship. The championship, the Japan Series, takes place in October and, like the MLB World Series, is a seven-game contest.

The Japanese style of play is focused on speed and strategy over getting big hits at big times. If the first batter in an inning gets on base, the next batter will almost always try to bunt—even if he's the team's top slugger! This spirit of group harmony is called *wa* and is at the heart of Japanese society.

Baseball practice begins at a young age.

*The game spread, like a fire in a dry field, in summer, all over the country, and some months afterwards, even children in primary schools in the country far away from Tōkyō were to be seen playing with bats and balls.*

TSUNEO MATSUDAIRA

| | TEAM | CITY |
|---|---|---|
| A | Chiba Lotte Marines | Chiba |
| B | Chunichi Dragons | Nagoya |
| C | Fukuoka SoftBank Hawks | Fukuoka |
| D | Hanshin Tigers | Nishinomiya |
| E | Hiroshima Toyo Carp | Hiroshima |
| F | Hokkaido Nippon-Ham Fighters | Sapporo |
| G | Orix Buffaloes | Osaka |
| H | Saitama Seibu Lions | Tokorozawa |
| I | Tohoku Rakuten Golden Eagles | Sendai |
| J | Tokyo Yakult Swallows | Tokyo |
| K | Yokohama DeNA BayStars | Yokohama |
| L | Yomiuri Giants | Tokyo |

Ichiro Suzuki

Shohei Ohtani

## FAMOUS PLAYERS

*Fans in Japan follow their favorite players closely, even when those players leave to play in other countries. Ichiro Suzuki, for instance, had an outstanding career both in Japan and then in the U.S. In fact, Ichiro is considered a national hero back home. Today, fans almost can't believe the performance of Shohei Ohtani (Los Angeles Angels). Shohei excels at both pitching and hitting—a very rare achievement.*

## WORLD BASEBALL CLASSIC

*The World Baseball Classic is an international tournament featuring teams from around the world made up of each country's best players. Founded in 2005, the first competition took place in 2006. The purpose of the tournament is to show the talents of players in other countries, as well as to further the game around the world. In 2006, Japanese star pitcher Daisuke Matsuzaka was unbeatable. Soon after he introduced himself on the world stage, Daisuke received a multimillion-dollar contract to join the Boston Red Sox.*

## OCTOPUS, ANYONE?

*Being a fan at a Japanese baseball game means active and enthusiastic participation by everyone. Led by the home team's cheering squad, throughout the entire game, fans sing, chant slogans, and bang drums. And no one boos a bad call. For food choices, the stadiums offer many typical Japanese items—bento boxes with sushi and rice balls, noodle bowls, and a dish named tokoyaki (fried dough balls filled with octopus—shown right).*

# SOUTH KOREA

## HOW BASEBALL ARRIVED

In the late 19th century, an American missionary named Philip Gillett was sent to Korea. While he was there, he introduced the local youth to the game of baseball (as well as basketball). Later, when the Japanese took control of the country, baseball there spread even farther. (Baseball in Japan had already taken hold and was becoming widely popular.) As the Korean players improved their skills, they regularly faced Japanese teams. After World War II, the country was split in two (North and South). Now, it was the South Koreans who continued their hunger for the game.

A baseball team plays during the 1920 Korean National Sports Festival.

## WHAT IT'S LIKE TODAY

The first season of the Korea Baseball Organization (KBO) League was played in 1982. Today, ten teams play 144 games each over a season that lasts from May through October. Unlike the MLB, games can end in a tie (only three extra innings are allowed) and all teams use the designated hitter.

At the end of the season, the top five teams enter into the playoffs. The playoff structure is truly unique, though. The number-four and -five seeded teams play first, and the winner then faces number three. That winner then faces the number-two team. The winner of that series then earns the right to play the number-one seed in the KBO Korean Series. But there's more to know. Playoff games have a fifteen-inning limit. If a game ends in a tie, the entire game is played over.

A U.S. Air Force officer teaches baseball to a Korean youth.

A BRIEF TIMELINE OF BASEBALL IN SOUTH KOREA

1880s: American missionaries introduce baseball to Korea.
1896: U.S. Marines play an exhibition game.

1927: Local Korean teams begin participating in the Japanese Intercity Baseball Tournament.

1850   1860   1870   1880   1890   1900   1910   1920   1930

## Team / City Table

| | TEAM | CITY |
|---|---|---|
| A | Doosan Bears | Seoul |
| B | Hanwha Eagles | Daejeon |
| C | Kia Tigers | Gwangju |
| D | Kiwoom Heroes | Seoul |
| E | KT Wiz | Suwon, Gyeonggi |
| F | LG Twins | Seoul |
| G | Lotte Giants | Busan |
| H | NC Dinos | Changwon, Gyeongnam |
| I | Samsung Lions | Daegu |
| J | SSG Landers | Incheon |

## PITCHING SENSATION

Korean pitcher Chan Ho Park made history in 1994 when he became the first Korean player to join the MLB. He went on to have a long career and still holds the record for most wins by an Asian pitcher. He earned such high esteem in Korea that when he pitched for the KBO's Hanwha Eagles during his final professional season, batters bowed when they approached the plate. Since his arrival, more than two dozen South Korean players have made it to the MLB. Today, look for Ji-man Choi (Tampa Bay Rays) and Hyun-jin Ryu (Toronto Blue Jays).

Fried chicken is a stadium favorite!

## DRUMROLL, PLEASE...

KBO games are known for being noisy. Fans cheer loudly while beating on drums and chanting their team's fight songs. Also, cheerleaders play the home team's cheer songs whenever their player is at bat. Every team and every player has their own song. As for food, Korean stadiums offer many options, from fast-food chains (KFC, Burger King) to local dishes such as pork barbecue. But the most popular stadium food is fried chicken. Some fans even admit that they go to games for the food and the party atmosphere.

## KOREA FIRST

The league limits the number of foreign-born players to just three per team. And no two can be on the field at the same time. Nonetheless, the KBO is popular with players from the MLB, as well as from Venezuela and the Dominican Republic.

---

1945: Korea splits into two.
1950–1953: Korean War.

1982: First league (KBO) is formed.

2000: South Korea wins bronze medal at Summer Olympics.

1940  1950  1960  1970  1980  1990  2000  2010  2020  2030

# AUSTRALIA

| QUICK STATS | YEAR STARTED | NUMBER OF TEAMS | PERMANENT STADIUMS | |
|---|---|---|---|---|
| 🇦🇺 | 1850s | 8 | 8 | |

## HOW BASEBALL ARRIVED

The history of how baseball arrived in Australia is cloudy. As early as the 1850s, newspaper stories mention baseball clubs facing each other. Regardless, it was a tour of American players led by Albert Spalding that really caught the locals' attention. Spalding was a former pitcher who turned his attention to business. In 1888, he led a group of American players on a world tour in order to promote baseball outside the U.S. The games in Australia attracted large crowds. Baseball's popularity continued to grow throughout the 1900s as amateur teams sprouted up around the country. Then, in 1989, the Australian Baseball League formed. The purpose of the league was to bring the teams together and raise their status to the level of professional. The league lasted for only ten years, however.

Above: An Australian baseball team poses for a photo in 1945. Left: Australian Archbishop Daniel Mannix throws the first pitch at a game in New York.

## WHAT IT'S LIKE TODAY

In 2009, after struggling for a decade, the Australian Baseball Federation joined forces with MLB to form a new Australian Baseball League (ABL). (The federation governs all amateur and professional baseball in Australia.) The newly formed league has eight teams, and each team plays forty games. The season takes place during the Southern Hemisphere summer, meaning that it runs November through January. The top five teams enter the playoffs—the fourth and fifth seeds play a wild-card game. The top four teams then face each other to determine who goes to the championship. Finally, the winner of the championship is awarded a trophy named the Claxton Shield (shown left).

The Sydney Cricket Grounds hosted the New York Giants and Chicago White Sox for an exhibition game in 1914. Australian teams now have their own stadiums and don't have to convert cricket pitches into baseball fields!

| TEAM | CITY |
|------|------|
| A Adelaide Giants | West Beach, South Australia |
| B Auckland Tuatara | Auckland, New Zealand |
| C Brisbane Bandits | Newmarket, Queensland |
| D Canberra Cavalry | Canberra, Australian Capital Territory |
| E Geelong-Korea | Geelong, Victoria |
| F Melbourne Aces | Laverton, Victoria |
| G Perth Heat | Perth, Western Australia |
| H Sydney Blue Sox | Sydney, New South Wales |

## WHO WAS SPALDING?

*Albert (A. G.) Spalding was a league-leading pitcher for the Boston Red Stockings. He joined the team in 1871. During his pitching career, Spalding used a baseball that he created himself. The ball later became the official baseball of the Major Leagues. (Spalding also created the first American football, in 1887, and the first basketball, in 1894.) Spalding was also one of the first players to use a glove to protect his catching hand. He went on to create the very first baseball glove. While he was still a pitcher, he and the owner of the Chicago White Stockings, William Hulbert, formed the National League of Professional Baseball Clubs. We now know this simply as the National League.*

## FIRST WOMAN PLAYER

*In January 2022, history was made when a young woman pitched in a professional ABL game. Genevieve Beacom, a seventeen-year-old, took the mound for the Melbourne Aces. She pitched a scoreless sixth inning and gave up no hits. Australian rules allow players to remain amateurs, even if they pitch at the major league level. Because of that, Genevieve hopes to continue her career by playing college baseball in the U.S.*

## COUSINS

Because the ABL has close ties to MLB, it's common for American minor leaguers to join Australian teams. The Perth Heat, for instance, have a close relationship with the Tampa Bay Rays and regularly feature top Rays prospects. Also, since the Australian season takes place over their summertime, playing there is particularly attractive. As for local players having a career in MLB, only thirty-three have reached the majors. Look for Liam Hendricks (Chicago White Sox). Liam made his first All-Star Game appearance in 2019.

Girls play baseball in Brisbane, Australia, in 1940.

1989: Australian Baseball League is formed.

2004: Australia wins silver in Summer Olympics.

2009: A new Australian Baseball League is launched with MLB.

1940  1950  1960  1970  1980  1990  2000  2010  2020  2030

# LITTLE LEAGUE

| | YEAR STARTED | NUMBER OF TEAMS | NUMBER OF COUNTRIES | |
|---|---|---|---|---|
| | 1939 | 200,000+ | 80+ | |

## HOW IT STARTED

One day in 1938, a man named Carl Stotz was playing catch with his nephews, when he tripped over a lilac bush. His frustration at not having a place for the kids to play ball led to an idea. Carl was a huge baseball fan. He recognized that sports, especially baseball, taught many important lessons, including fair play, teamwork, and community. Baseball had been around for a long time, but there was no organized program aimed at kids. So, Carl approached several local businesses with the idea of a youth baseball league. He founded the Little League in 1939 in Williamsport, Pennsylvania. Starting with just three teams and thirty players, the organized league was a big success. In fewer than ten years, forty-seven teams took the field.

The first leagues outside the United States were formed in 1950 on each side of the Panama Canal. Similar to the way in which professional baseball came to that country, the canal workers were excited to form teams for their kids. All over the world, parents and kids were eager to put on uniforms, just like the professionals.

## LITTLE LEAGUE WORLD SERIES

The following countries have participated in the Little League World Series.

- Aruba
- Australia
- Belgium
- Canada
- Curaçao
- Czech Republic
- Dominican Republic
- France
- Germany
- Greece
- Guam
- Italy
- Japan
- Mexico
- Netherlands
- Nicaragua
- Northern Mariana Islands
- Panama
- Philippines
- Poland
- Puerto Rico
- Russia
- Saudi Arabia
- South Korea
- Spain
- Turkey
- Uganda
- Venezuela

## WHAT IT'S LIKE TODAY

Today, Little League Baseball has 200,000 teams and is played in more than eighty countries. Teams are organized locally and then into regions—eight in the U.S. and eight for the rest of the world. Each season, the teams compete to see who will go to their Regional Tournament. The regional winners then go on to see who's the best in the world— to the Little League World Series. The regional winners are divided into two brackets (U.S. and International). The champions of each bracket then face each other in the Little League World Series Championship Game. The championship is held at the end of August in Williamsport, Pennsylvania, the birthplace of Little League.

Little League World Series underway in Williamsport, Pennsylvania.

**A BRIEF TIMELINE OF LITTLE LEAGUE**

1939: Carl Stotz founds Little League Baseball.

| 1850 | 1860 | 1870 | 1880 | 1890 | 1900 | 1910 | 1920 | 1930 |

# AN INTERNATIONAL SENSATION

Both at home and abroad, Little League Baseball has been an important launching pad for many of today's stars. Indeed, more than thirty members of the Baseball Hall of Fame got their start playing in the Little League. In addition to teaching the skills of the game and, frankly, being fun, Little League can be an opportunity for young players across the globe to show their talents. Here are just a few of the players who have had success in both Little League and MLB: Cody Bellinger (U.S.), Daisuke Matsuzaka (Japan), Wilson Alvarez (Venezuela), Jurickson Profar (Curaçao), Ruben Tejada (Panama), and Yusmeiro Petit (Venezuela). Speaking of Yusmeiro, he's the only player to ever win both the Little League World Series and the MLB World Series.

> *"Little League Baseball is a very good thing because it keeps the parents off the streets."*
>
> **—YOGI BERRA**

Then Secretary of State Condoleezza Rice stands with a Little League team in Chile.

## 'MAZING MO'NE

*Mo'ne Davis became the first female player to win a game as a pitcher in the Little League Baseball World Series. In the 2014 series, she threw fourteen strikeouts and allowed only three earned runs. In total, twenty girls have played in the Little League Baseball World Series.*

## GIRLS IN LITTLE LEAGUE

*At first, girls were not allowed to play in Little League. The organization feared they would be injured. After facing numerous lawsuits, in 1974 the league finally gave in and allowed girls to play. But one girl secretly snuck in years earlier. In 1950, Kathryn Johnston (shown left) cut off her braids, tucked her hair inside her cap, and won a spot on the local team. She went by the nickname "Tubby" so no one would know. By the time her coach and teammates found out, she had proved that she should keep playing.*

# SOURCES

## UNITED STATES

Martinez, Hiram. "An Edge: Spanish-Speaking Managers." ESPN, September 19, 2012. https://www.espn.com/mlb/story/_/page/OneNation-MLB120919/major-league-managers-speak-spanish-bring-competitive-edge-game.

"MLB International." MLB.com, n.d. https://www.mlb.com/international.

Rothenberg, Matt. "Pro Baseball Began in Cincinnati in 1869." Baseball Hall of Fame, n.d. https://baseballhall.org/discover/pro-baseball-began-in-cincinnati-in-1869.

Thompson, Bill. "The Negro Leagues and Latin America Are Intertwined Forever." Beyond the Box Score, February 12, 2021. https://www.beyondtheboxscore.com/2021/2/12/22268714/negro-leagues-latin-america-history-winter-leagues-jorge-pasquel-rafael-trujillo-satchel-paige.

## CUBA

Moist, John. "Touring the Ballparks of Cuba." Ballpark Digest - Chronicling the Business and Culture of Baseball Ballparks--MLB, MiLB, College, January 28, 2015. https://ballparkdigest.com/201110174264/minor-league-baseball/visits/touring-the-ballparks-of-cuba.

"Cuban National League." Cuban National League - BR Bullpen, n.d. https://www.baseball-reference.com/bullpen/Cuban_National_League.

"Latin Americans in Major League Baseball through the First Years of the 21st Century." Encyclopædia Britannica, n.d. https://www.britannica.com/topic/Latin-Americans-in-Major-League-Baseball-910675.

Welle, Deutsche. "Why Cuban Baseball Players Fled Their Country." Accessed February 24, 2022. https://www.dw.com/en/why-cuban-baseball-players-fled-their-country/a-59417825.

Brioso, Cesar. "Cuban Stars Dot Rosters of Teams in MLB Playoffs, and Now They Can Shine on Biggest Stage." USA Today, October 5, 2021. https://www.usatoday.com/story/sports/mlb/2021/10/04/mlb-playoffs-cuban-stars-white-sox-astros-rays/5820133001/.

"Industriales." Wikipedia. Wikimedia Foundation, October 17, 2021. https://en.wikipedia.org/wiki/Industriales.

"Cuban League." Wikipedia. Wikimedia Foundation, February 21, 2022. https://en.wikipedia.org/wiki/Cuban_League.

## COLOMBIA

"Colombia." Colombia - BR Bullpen, n.d. https://www.baseball-reference.com/bullpen/Colombia.

"Liga Colombiana De Béisbol Profesional." Liga Colombiana de Béisbol Profesional - BR Bullpen, n.d. https://www.baseball-reference.com/bullpen/Liga_Colombiana_de_B%C3%A9isbol_Profesional.

## NICARAGUA

Guy, Jack. "How Did Baseball Become Nicaragua's National Sport?" The Culture Trip, April 27, 2018. https://theculturetrip.com/central-america/nicaragua/articles/how-did-baseball-become-nicaraguas-national-sport/.

"Nicaragua Blog: Days 2-11 Playing Ball in a Baseball Crazy Country." Augustana University Athletics, n.d. https://goaugie.com/news/2015/1/24/BB_01241525201.

"Nicaraguan Professional Baseball League." Wikipedia. Wikimedia Foundation, January 31, 2022. https://en.wikipedia.org/wiki/Nicaraguan_Professional_Baseball_League.

"History of Baseball in Nicaragua." Wikiwand, n.d. https://www.wikiwand.com/en/History_of_baseball_in_Nicaragua.

## PANAMA

"Liga Profesional De Béisbol De Panamá." Liga Profesional de Béisbol de Panamá - BR Bullpen, n.d. https://www.baseball-reference.com/bullpen/Liga_Profesional_de_B%C3%A9isbol_de_Panam%C3%A1.

Thorn, John. "Panama Baseball: A Brief History." Medium. Our Game, January 25, 2017. https://ourgame.mlblogs.com/panama-baseball-a-brief-history-e601281f1c8d.

## DOMINICAN REPUBLIC

"Baseball." GoDominicanRepublic.com, August 4, 2018. https://www.godominicanrepublic.com/about-dr/baseball/.

"The Dominican Republic and the United States: A Baseball History." Origins, n.d. https://origins.osu.edu/article/dominican-republic-and-united-states-baseball-history.

## PUERTO RICO

"Puerto Rico's 2021-2022 Winter Baseball League." PRDayTrips Travel Planning Guide, n.d. https://www.puertoricodaytrips.com/winter-baseball/.

## ITALY

DW Akademie: Welle, Deutsche. "The Home of Baseball - in Italy," n.d. https://www.dw.com/en/the-home-of-baseball-in-italy/a-4832086.

Angelini, Andrea, Jana Godshall, Matthew Burgos, Sara Belletti, and Sophia Rita Jadda. "Yes, We Baseball." Italics Magazine, March 21, 2020. https://italicsmag.com/2020/03/21/yes-we-baseball-in-italy/.

"Italy's Top Baseball League to Expand to 33 Teams, Opens 7 May." wbsc.org, n.d. https://www.wbsc.org/news/italys-top-baseball-league-to-expand-to-33-teams-opens-7-may.

## JAPAN

"10 Things You Didn't Know about Japanese Baseball." Jugs Sports, n.d. https://jugssports.com/blog/10-things-you-didnt-know-about-japanese-baseball/.

"Baseball Is the National Game in Japan," n.d. http://research.sabr.org/journals/basbeall-is-the-national-game-in-japan.

## SOUTH KOREA

Huddleston, Tom. "No MLB? Korean Baseball Is in Full Swing-Here's What You Need to Know, from KBO Cheerleaders to Bat-Flipping." CNBC, May 25, 2020. https://www.cnbc.com/2020/05/25/espn-is-airing-korean-baseball-what-you-need-to-know-about-the-kbo.html.

The Korea Herald, n.d. http://www.koreaherald.com/.

## VENEZUELA

"Venezuelan League." Venezuelan League - BR Bullpen, n.d. https://www.baseball-reference.com/bullpen/Venezuelan_League.

"Miguel Cabrera." Encyclopædia Britannica. Accessed February 24, 2022. https://www.britannica.com/biography/Miguel-Cabrera-baseball-player.

Cremonesi, Rafael Rojas. "Why Are Venezuelans so Crazy about Beisbol?" Caracas Chronicles, January 2, 2016. https://www.caracaschronicles.com/2016/01/02/why-are-venezuelans-so-crazy-about-beisbol/.

"All-Latino Baseball Team: The Best All-Time Lineup of Players Born in Venezuela." USA Today, September 24, 2021. https://www.usatoday.com/story/sports/mlb/2021/09/24/best-venezuelan-baseball-players-all-time-lineup-venezuela/8362768002/.

## AUSTRALIA

Thorn, John. "Australian Baseball: A Brief History." Medium. Our Game, July 27, 2018. https://ourgame.mlblogs.com/australian-baseball-a-brief-history-54e1cadfddb1.

Sterling, Wayne. "Genevieve Beacom Becomes First Woman to Pitch in the Australian Baseball League." CNN, January 9, 2022. https://www.cnn.com/2022/01/09/sport/genevieve-beacom-abl-pitch-spt-intl/index.html.

## LITTLE LEAGUE

"Little League." Encyclopædia Britannica, n.d. https://www.britannica.com/topic/Little-League.

Little League. "Little League® Fast Facts." Little League, January 25, 2022. https://www.littleleague.org/little-league-fast-facts.

"15 Major Facts about Little League Baseball." Mental Floss, September 15, 2016. https://www.mentalfloss.com/article/85076/15-major-facts-about-little-league-baseball.

"Small Ball: Famous Little League World Series Alumni." Yardbarker, March 11, 2021. https://www.yardbarker.com/mlb/articles/small_ball_famous_little_league_world_series_alumni/s1__22679773#slide_5.

# IMAGE CREDITS

## ABOUT THE AUTHORS

**CHRIS SINGLETON** is an inspirational speaker and former professional baseball player who travels the country as a student achievement specialist. Chris has spoken to over 100,000 students and teachers across the nation and has helped thousands of students and teachers overcome hardships and excel in the classroom. Chris's speech on overcoming hate with love has been seen or shared millions of times and has gotten him featured on Lifetime, ESPN E:60, USA Today, CNN, and Fox News. Chris is a proud father of his sons, CJ and Caden, and a proud husband to his high school sweetheart, Mariana. He can be found online at www.chrissingleton.com/bookings and on social media at @csingleton_2.

**DEAN BURRELL** is a decades-long baseball fan, having learned the game by watching the greats at Candlestick Park in San Francisco. Living in the Bay Area, Dean is fortunate enough to have access to two local Major League teams and has been known to sneak out of work to attend day games (but don't tell his boss).

⭐ If you liked this book, please leave a review online at your favorite retailer. Honest reviews spread the word about Bushel & Peck—and help us make better books, too!

💟 www.bushelandpeckbooks.com/pages/nominate-a-school-or-organization

C. ROYER P. BEBE

## ABOUT BUSHEL & PECK BOOKS

Bushel & Peck Books is a children's publishing house with a special mission. Through our Book-for-Book Promise™, we donate one book to kids in need for every book we sell. Our beautiful books are given to kids through schools, libraries, local neighborhoods, shelters, nonprofits, and also to many selfless organizations who are working hard to make a difference. So thank you for purchasing this book! Because of you, another book will find itself in the hands of a child who needs it most.

## WHY LITERACY MATTERS

We can't solve every problem in the world, but we believe children's books can help. Illiteracy is linked to many of the world's greatest challenges, including crime, school dropout rates, and drug use. Yet impressively, just the presence of books in a home can be a leg up for struggling kids. According to one study, "Children growing up in homes with many books get three years more schooling than children from bookless homes, independent of their parents' education, occupation, and class. This is as great an advantage as having university educated rather than unschooled parents, and twice the advantage of having a professional rather than an unskilled father."[1]

Unfortunately, many children in need find themselves without adequate access to age-appropriate books. One study found that low-income neighborhoods have, in some U.S. cities, only one book for every three hundred kids (compared to thirteen books for every one child in middle-income neighborhoods).[2]

With our Book-for-Book Promise™, Bushel & Peck Books is putting quality children's books into the hands of as many kids as possible. We hope these books bring an increased interest in reading and learning, and with that, a greater chance for future success.

1    M.D.R. Evans, Jonathan Kelley, Joanna Sikora & Donald J. Treiman. Family scholarly culture and educational success: Books and schooling in 27 nations. *Research in Social Stratification and Mobility*. Volume 28, Issue 2, 2010. 171-197.
2    Neuman, S.B. & D. Celano (2006). The knowledge gap: Effects of leveling the playing field for low- and middle-income children. *Reading Research Quarterly*, 176-201.